HOLIDAY JOKES & SWEET TREATS

GROUNDHOG DAY GIGGLES & GOODIES

Anna Anderhagen

Consulting Editor, Diane Craig, MA/Reading Specialist

Super Sandcastle

An Imprint of Abdo Publishing
abdobooks.com

abdobooks.com

Published by Abdo Publishing, a division of ABDO, PO Box 398166, Minneapolis, Minnesota 55439.

Printed in the United States of America, North Mankato, Minnesota
102024
012025

Design: Layne Halvorsen, Mighty Media, Inc.
Production: Mighty Media, Inc.
Editor: Liz Salzmann
Cover Photographs: Mighty Media, Inc. (recipe photos); Shutterstock Images
Interior Photographs: Adobe Stock, pp. 4 (hedgehog, badger), 8 (pretzels),10–11 (hand & tweezers), 12 (hands), 13 (containers, washing plate), 20 (groundhog), 22 (groundhog), 24 (groundhogs), 30 (car); Mighty Media, Inc. (recipe photos), pp. 10, 11, 14, 15, 16, 17, 18, 19, 20, 21, 22, 23, 24, 25, 26, 27, 29; Shutterstock Images, pp. 1 (rolling pin), 4 (groundhog), 5 (groundhog & grass), 6 (all), 7 (child), 8 (almond bark, raspberries, strawberries), 8–9 (coconut, jelly beans, doughnuts), 9 (all), 11 (raspberry), 14 (groundhog), 16 (pretzels, groundhog), 28–29 (child), 29 (rolling pin, plate), 30 (calendar, groundhog), 31 (child)
Design Elements: Shutterstock Images (abstract doodles, kitchen utensil doodles)

Library of Congress Control Number: 2024938352

Publisher's Cataloging-in-Publication Data
Names: Anderhagen, Anna, author.
Title: Groundhog day giggles & goodies / by Anna Anderhagen
Description: Minneapolis, Minnesota : ABDO Publishing, 2025 | Series: Holiday jokes & sweet treats | Includes online resources and index.
Identifiers: ISBN 9781098295189 (lib. bdg.) | ISBN 9798384915232 (ebook)
Subjects: LCSH: Jokes--Juvenile literature. | Groundhog Day--Juvenile literature. | Holidays--Juvenile literature. | Snack foods--Juvenile literature. | Cooking--Juvenile literature.
Classification: DDC 398.7--dc23

TO ADULT HELPERS

The sweet treats in this series are fun and simple. There are just a few things to remember to keep kids safe. Creating some treats requires the use of hot objects. Also, kids may be using messy materials, such as food coloring. Make sure they protect their clothes and work surfaces. Review the projects before starting and be ready to assist when necessary.

Super Sandcastle™ books are created by a team of professional educators, reading specialists, and content developers around five essential components—phonemic awareness, phonics, vocabulary, text comprehension, and fluency—to assist young readers as they develop reading skills and strategies and increase their general knowledge. All books are written, reviewed, and leveled for guided reading and early reading intervention programs for use in shared, guided, and independent reading and writing activities to support a balanced approach to literacy instruction.

Contents

GROUNDHOG DAY

Do you think animals can **predict** the weather? That's what Groundhog Day is all about. It's the day when people watch a groundhog come out of its **burrow**. If the groundhog goes right back in, people say it saw its shadow. This means there will be six more weeks of winter. If the groundhog stays outside, spring will come early!

This **tradition** started in Europe hundreds of years ago. In the 1700s, German **immigrants** brought it to Pennsylvania. In Germany, they had watched badgers and **hedgehogs**. There weren't many of them in Pennsylvania. But there were a lot of groundhogs! So, groundhogs became the weather predictors.

The most famous groundhog is Punxsutawney Phil. Each year, more than 30,000 fans come to Punxsutawney, Pennsylvania, on Groundhog Day. Other Groundhog Day activities include parades, dressing up, and gathering to celebrate the changing seasons.

Holiday Hoots!

Which animal takes up a lot of room?

A groundhog.

How does the groundhog know when to look for his shadow?

When he is told to gopher it.

Where do groundhogs with magical powers go to school?

Hogwarts.

What is a groundhog's favorite drink?

Hole milk.

What's always found on the ground but never gets dirty?

A shadow.

What is a groundhog's favorite weather?

Ground fog.

What do puppies celebrate on February 2?

Ground-Dog Day.

Why is it not fun to watch TV with groundhogs?

They hog the remote.

Why did the groundhog wear sunglasses on Groundhog Day?

He didn't want his shadow to recognize him.

Sweet Materials

Here are some of the ingredients and tools you will need to make the treats in this book.

Ingredients

- bear graham cookies
- brown candies
- candy eyes
- chocolate almond bark
- chocolate cookie crumbs
- chocolate iced doughnuts
- chocolate pudding cups
- chocolate sprinkles
- coconut flakes
- colorful candy-covered chocolates
- fresh fruit
- frosting
- graham crackers
- green food coloring
- jelly beans
- large chocolate cookies
- light-colored mini cookies
- Milano cookies
- mini chocolate chips
- mini marshmallows
- Nutter Butter cookies
- pepitas
- powdered sugar
- pretzel sticks
- slivered almonds
- snack mix ingredients
- soft caramel squares

Tools

- baking sheet
- bowls
- marker
- measuring cups
- microwave-safe bowl
- parchment paper
- scissors
- sealable plastic bag
- serving plate
- sharp knife & cutting board
- small pieces of paper
- tape
- toothpicks

Who didn't come to the candy party on time?

Choco-late.

Can February March?

No, but April May!

Frosting Tips & Tricks

Using Frosting to Attach Items

Attaching items such as candy pieces with frosting is a fun way to decorate treats. Here are some tips and tricks to make sure decorations stay in place.

- Spread a thin layer of frosting to stick items to. This provides a smooth surface so they stick better.
- Add items quickly, before the frosting dries.
- Press the items into the frosting gently but firmly. Don't press so hard that frosting **oozes** up around the items..

What do you call a dog that gets covered with frosting?

A pup-cake.

- Use a toothpick or **tweezers** to place small items. This helps keep your fingers from touching the frosting.
- After attaching items, allow at least 10 minutes for the frosting to set. This helps the items stick better. You could also put the treats in the refrigerator to help the frosting set.

Knock, knock!
Who's there?
Grover.
Grover who?
Grover there and get me a cookie.

Treats Prep

Be Safe

* Ask an adult for permission to use kitchen tools and ingredients.
* Ask an adult to help you use the microwave.
* Ask an adult for help when handling sharp or hot objects.
* Clean up spills right away.

What does Punxsutawney Phil call his laundry?

Hogwash.

Get Ready!

* Wash your hands.
* Clean your work surface before you start.
* Read the list of tools and ingredients for the sweet treat you are making. Set out everything you will need.
* Read the whole recipe at least once before you start.

When You Are Finished

- Let hot treats cool completely.
- Put all the ingredients and tools away.
- Store leftover ingredients to use later.
- Wash all the dishes and cooking tools.
- Clean your work surface.
- Wash your hands before you eat your sweet treats!

Groundhog Pop-Ups

Who leaps tall buildings with a single bound?

Super hog!

Ingredients

- coconut flakes
- green food coloring
- mini marshmallows
- brown candies
- Nutter Butter cookies
- candy eyes
- chocolate pudding cups

Tools

- measuring cups
- bowl
- fork
- sharp knife & cutting board
- table knife

POP!

1. Put 1 cup of coconut flakes in a bowl. Add three drops of green food coloring. Mix well with a fork. This is the grass.
2. Cut mini marshmallows into smaller pieces. These are the groundhogs' teeth. Cut up some brown candies for ears.
3. Pull the cookies apart. Use a table knife to scrape off the filling. The cookies are the groundhogs' bodies.

4. Use the filling to attach features to the cookies. Add two candy eyes, a brown candy nose, two marshmallow teeth, and two brown candy ears to each cookie.
5. Push a groundhog into each chocolate pudding cup. Sprinkle some green coconut grass on top. Share them with friends on Groundhog Day!

What is in the middle of a coconut?

The letter o!

Groundhog Trail Mix

How does Punxsutawney Phil greet his parents?

With hogs and kisses.

Ingredients

- 4 2-ounce squares of chocolate almond bark
- candy eyes
- brown candies
- slivered almonds
- snack mix ingredients (cereal, pretzels, dried fruit, nuts)

Tools

CRUNCHY

- baking sheet
- parchment paper
- sharp knife & cutting board
- microwave-safe bowl
- spoon
- sealable plastic bag
- scissors

- large bowl
- silicone spatula
- small serving bowls

1. Line the baking sheet with parchment paper.
2. Cut the almond bark into small **chunks**. Put it in a microwave-safe bowl. Microwave for 20 seconds at a time. Stir after each time. Repeat until it is creamy and smooth.
3. Put the melted almond bark in a plastic bag. Cut off the tip of one corner of the bag.
4. **Squeeze** the bag to make triangles of almond bark on the baking sheet. These are the groundhogs' heads.
5. Working quickly before the almond bark cools, add features to each head. Add candy eyes, a brown candy nose, and two slivered almonds for teeth.

Continued on the next page.

How do groundhogs feel about Groundhog Day?

They dig it, of course!

6. Put the baking sheet in the refrigerator for about 30 minutes.
7. Combine the snack mix ingredients in a large bowl.
8. Put some snack mix in each serving bowl. Top each one with a chocolate groundhog. Invite some friends over for a Groundhog Day snack!

Why are groundhogs good storytellers?

They have many tales of shadowy adventures!

COOL!
Knock, knock!
Who's there?
Jess.
Jess Who?
Jess me and my shadow.

Groundhog Grahams

What do you call it when a bunch of strawberries play rock music?
A jam session.

Ingredients

- fresh fruit (strawberries, raspberries, blueberries, grapes)
- pretzel sticks
- bear graham cookies
- white frosting
- graham crackers
- chocolate cookie crumbs
- mini chocolate chips

Tools

- sharp knife & cutting board
- table knife
- spoon

1. Cut the fruit into small flower-petal shapes. Break pretzel sticks into shorter pieces for flower stems. Cut the heads off some bear grahams.
2. Spread white frosting on one side of a graham cracker. Add cookie crumbs along one edge of the cracker for dirt.
3. Use fruit and pretzels to create flowers growing out of the dirt.
4. Use frosting to stick a mini chocolate chip to the nose of a bear graham head. Now it's a groundhog head.

5. Place the groundhog head so it's peeking out of the dirt.
6. Repeat steps 2 through 5 to make more groundhog grahams to share with your friends

What do you call a flower that runs on electricity?

A power plant!

Cheeky Groundhog Cookies

Why do basketball players love cookies?
Because they can dunk them.

Ingredients

- chocolate frosting
- large chocolate cookies
- light-colored mini cookies (gingersnaps or vanilla wafers work well)
- chocolate sprinkles
- jelly beans
- candy eyes
- pepitas
- brown candies

Tool

- table knife

1. Spread chocolate frosting on a large chocolate cookie.
2. Press two small cookies into the frosting. These are the groundhog's cheeks.
3. Put chocolate sprinkles above the cheeks for fur.
4. Use small amounts of frosting to add a jelly bean nose, two candy eyes, two pepitas for teeth, and two brown candies for ears.
5. Repeat steps 1 through 4 to make more cheeky groundhog cookies. Give them to friends and family members on Groundhog Day!

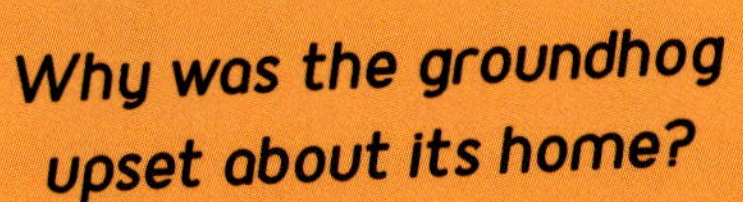

It was having a bad lair day.

Groundhog Doughnuts

Why did the doughnut visit the dentist?

It needed a chocolate filling.

Ingredients

- 6 soft caramel squares
- Milano cookies
- brown candies
- candy eyes
- colorful candy-covered chocolates
- chocolate iced doughnuts
- powdered sugar

Tools

- microwave-safe bowl
- spoon
- small pieces of paper
- marker
- toothpicks
- tape

YAY!

1. Put the caramel squares in a microwave-safe bowl. Microwave for 10 seconds at a time. Stir after each time. Repeat until the caramel is soft enough to **mold**.
2. Take a pinch of the warm caramel. Press it flat. Place the caramel near one end of a Milano cookie. This is the groundhog's face.
3. Push a brown candy into the caramel for the nose. Add candy eyes above the nose.
4. Use two more pinches of the warm caramel to stick colorful candy-covered chocolates to the edge for ears.
5. Sprinkle powdered sugar over a **doughnut**.

Continued on the next page.

6. Push the groundhog cookie into the center hole of the **doughnut**.
7. Repeat steps 2 through 6 to make more groundhog doughnuts.
8. Make **festive** signs for the doughnuts. Write messages on small pieces of paper. Tape them to toothpicks. Stick the signs into the doughnuts.
9. Enjoy them on Groundhog Day morning as you wait to hear whether the groundhog saw its shadow!

Knock, knock!

Who's there?

Icing.

Icing who?

Icing so loud the neighbors can hear me!

A-DOUGH-RABLE!
HAPPY groundhog day!
What is a groundhog's favorite color?
Ma-hog-any.

Keep Creating!

You've made some **delicious** treats with the recipes in this book! Hopefully you had some laughs with your friends too. But could you make any of the recipes differently? Could you use different ingredients? Or can you think of your own Groundhog Day treat?

Do you or a friend have a nut **allergy**? Try making the Groundhog Pop-Ups with Milano cookies instead of Nutter Butter cookies. Then use frosting to stick on the eyes, ears, nose, and teeth.

Does a treat include an ingredient you don't like? Get creative! Find something else to use that you do like. For example, you could use slivered almonds or sunflower seeds instead of pepitas for the Cheeky Groundhog Cookie teeth.

Why was Phil kicked off the Punxsutawney soccer team?

For being a ball hog.

Just use your imagination to keep creating!

Last Laughs

Where do sick groundhogs go?

The hogs-pital.

What do you call a groundhog who drives in the center of the road?

A road hog.

How many seconds are in a year?

Twelve. January second, February second, March second...

What is a groundhog's camper called?

A wheel-burrow.

What's green and jumps out of a hole on February 2?

A ground frog.

What did the groundhog say when a wolf grabbed its tail?

That's the end of me.

What do you call a pig with no legs?

A ground hog.

How do groundhogs smell?

With their noses.

What did the groundhog say when it saw its shadow?

Nothing! Groundhogs can't speak.

Glossary

allergy – a sickness caused by touching, breathing, or eating certain things.

burrow – an animal's underground home.

chunk – a short, thick piece or lump of something.

delicious – very pleasing to taste.

doughnut – a fried, usually round cake often eaten for breakfast.

festive – cheerful, bright, and exciting.

hedgehog – an animal that has sharp spines on its back and can roll up into a spiny ball when scared.

immigrant – someone who has left his or her home and settled in a new country.

mold – to work and press into shape with your fingers.

ooze – to flow or spread slowly.

predict – to say something is going to happen before it does. Someone who does this is a predictor.

squeeze – to press the sides of something together.

tradition – a belief or practice passed through a family or group of people.

tweezers – a small tool used to grasp or pull something.